Also by L. D. Hicks

Melania Trump: Elegance in the White House

Trump 45

L. D. HICKS

Post Hill
PRESS

A POST HILL PRESS BOOK
ISBN: 978-1-63758-165-0

Trump 45:
America's Greatest President
© 2021 by Post Hill Press
All Rights Reserved

Cover art by Cody Corcoran

Post Hill Press
New York • Nashville
posthillpress.com

Printed in Canada
1 2 3 4 5 6 7 8 9 10

To my beautiful wife Lisa, 852 and to my sister-in-law Gail,
huge Donald Trump fan!

A Summary of Donald Trump's Presidency

On November 19, 2016, Donald Trump and Mike Pence won the 2016 election, defeating Hillary Clinton in a massive upset, shocking half of the country and forcing many liberal Democrats into therapy. On election night, Republicans celebrated with glee while crestfallen faces on the left shrank from positivity to mortification. Hillary Clinton, the woman who would shatter the glass ceiling of American politics, the hope of progressives to continue the Obama legacy, was defeated by a hotel owner and reality television star.

Since the turn of the century, many Americans felt they had been under siege. Traditional American values had been under constant assault. Like the defenders of the Alamo, conservatives, blue collar workers, evangelicals, and average Americans watched in abject horror the rise of cancel culture, woke mobs, leftist politicians, and progressive media. Social media giants like Facebook, Twitter, and Reddit began silencing and shadowbanning conservative posts and comments. Every Republican president was smeared. Reagan was senile, George Bush was a wimp, and George W. Bush was stupid. A tradition going back as far as Dwight D. Eisenhower. Prayer was banned in schools, red tape and senseless regulations strangled infrastructure projects and new industry and drove the cost of fuel to new highs. Higher taxes and ridiculous union demands drove industries to move manufacturing plants overseas. Call centers and help desks were outsourced to India. Americans saw their way of life and prosperity begin to crumble. Young people were infantile and still living at home with their parents or earning degrees on the effects of underwater basket weaving or the effects of gender norms. Many people were angry, out of work, and saw no hope for the future. Conservatives and voters were frustrated by the continual flaccid responses of candidates and elected officials they voted into office. Oftentimes they would run for office on conservative values and once elected they would turn their coat to ooze their way into elite circles. People were desperate for a voice crying in the wilderness.

Trump voters are people who believe in the sanctity of life, freedom of speech and thought, the American family, and the history and traditions of the United States. Donald Trump stood up to the bullies, the cancellers, and the liberal media. The president stood up for those Americans longing for someone to stand up for them and not "fit in" or cowardly maintain the collegial politics of the old days as the left ripped them to shreds. Donald Trump became the defender of bedrock of America. The voice for the voiceless.

The slogan of Donald Trump's presidency was "*Make America Great Again*" and upon election he went straight to work. Immediately after assuming office, Trump withdrew the United States from the Trans-Pacific Partnership, a job-killing, China-boosting trade deal. Ten days after his inauguration, Trump issued Executive Order 13771, which required agencies to offset the cost of any new significant regulation with at least two deregulatory actions. It also established a regulatory budgeting system under which the Office of Management and Budget assigns to agencies a cap on the amount of incremental costs that will be allowed for the fiscal year. In 2019, the Budget office projected to free up almost $18 billion in regulatory costs. With the stroke of a pen, Donald Trump ripped the heart out of the regulatory system in Washington, D.C., and lit the fuse on a new explosive economy.

The Trump Administration also ended the soul-crushing North American Free Trade Agreement, a staple of RINO Republicans and another job killer. Instead, Trump negotiated a new Americas trade agreement expected to create over $50 billion in new economic activity and generate thousands of new jobs. Trump also signed an executive order making it government policy to buy American and hire American. The goal was to stop sending jobs overseas and to bring those sent away back to the U.S. from where they were cast aside with scarcely a care by the progressive elites.

During the first years of the Trump Administration, America gained over 7 million new jobs, middle class family income increased by nearly $6,000, and the unemployment rate shrank to unprecedented lows. More women and minority groups were working than ever before, and the bottom 50 percent of American households saw a 40 percent increase in net worth. Trump delivered on his promise to bring jobs, factories, and industries back to the USA. This coupled with taking a chainsaw to petty regulations threw a match on the fire of the American economy. Small businesses boomed, the S&P topped 30,000 in 2020, and rural America received access to funds and technology to boost production.

Trade deals were negotiated with countries in Asia, the European Union, India, and the Middle East. Digital trade was boosted with Japan, and agricultural imports were given special treatment in that country. Trump opened Japan for trade on par with Commodore Perry in the 1800s. The United States-Korea Free Trade Agreement was renegotiated which doubled the caps on imports of American vehicles. Astonishingly, the Phase One Trade Deal with China confronted pirated and counterfeit goods to protect the property rights of American ideas and trademarks. China agreed to purchase an additional $200 billion in American goods and opened access for more American goods and services into the country. To protect American business, the Trump administration took strong stances to make trade equal and put America first. Trump's doctrine holds that if one cannot care about his family, community, and country, then he cannot help his neighbor. A country should look inward first, strengthen itself, help increase the prosperity of its people, and then cooperate with the other nations in rising to the challenges of our century. "America First," he said on more than one occasion, "does not mean America Alone."[1]

To make the American farmer great again, the Trump Administration negotiated trade deals throughout the world in order to create access to untapped markets, enabling them to send produce and livestock overseas. Pork, poultry, wheat, eggs, and soybeans could now be traded without tariffs to Argentina, Brazil, South Korea, China, the European Union, and Guatemala. Twenty-eight billion dollars in aid went to farmers who had suffered from these unfair trade practices. The president indeed made farmers great again.

---

1   ("The True Legacy of Donald Trump" 2021)

The Tax Cuts and Jobs Act reformed the tax code and granted over $3.2 trillion in unprecedented tax relief. For the first time in decades, working class families had more money in their pockets, child tax credits were increased, and small businesses could deduct 20 percent of their income.

Under the Trump Administration, for the first time in seventy years, the United States now exported energy overseas. The country is now the number one nation in drilling, barreling, and piping natural gas and oil. Trump withdrew the United States from the Paris Agreement that nurtured our trade partners and penalized the country, effectively tying the United States's hand behind its back. The previous era's Clean Power Plan was scrapped and new standards were applied. The brakes were taken off the Keystone and Dakota Access Pipelines and the Arctic National Wildlife Refuge was finally opened to oil and gas leasing. The net effect was to lower costs on energy in the United States. Lower energy prices means it costs less to make, ship, and deliver products to grocery stores and American households. The price of a gallon of gas went down as well. This means lower prices for families at the pump, the grocery store, and the mall, putting more money in American's pockets. Standards of living rose and consumer confidence was high. America indeed was being made great once again.

Arguably, the greatest legacy of Donald Trump's presidency was the more conservative stamp on the judicial branch of government. Over previous decades, the Democrats had continuously used the courts to legislate policies the American people had rejected at the ballot box. A more conservative bench using judicial restraint would put a stop to this. Judicial appointments are confirmed for life, creating a long term legacy that would affect future generations of Americans. Donald Trump appointed three new Supreme Court Justices: Neil Gorsuch, Brett M. Kavanaugh, and Amy Coney Barrett. Not only did he appoint them, he stuck by them in the face of overwhelming leftist rage and scheming to smear each candidate until they were confirmed by the Senate. The president also nominated and confirmed 54 appellate court justices and 230 federal judges. This reset the balance on federal courts throughout the country. Trump's judges were also young, and lifetime appointments mean longer terms without having to be replaced. These judges will have an impact on the biggest issues the country faces: abortion, guns, and religious rights. Donald Trump has given the American people the chance to see the iron curtain of the culture wars raised and the hope of freedom to shine once again in the home of the brave.

The Trump Administration also undertook a colossal rebuilding of the United States military, and created the sixth branch of the armed forces—the United States Space Force. President Trump signed bills adding $2.2 trillion in defense spending. This included a pay raise for the men and women on the front lines of defending the United States. The funding modernized the country's aging nuclear forces and missile defenses. Cyber defenses were at the top of the list and elevated it into a major warfighting command. The Space Force is a new branch of the military alongside the army, air force, navy, and marines. The task of this new branch is to conduct military operations in outer space. The Space Force is the world's first and only independent force dedicated to protecting the United States's interests above the atmosphere.

In 2018, President Trump signed into law the VA MISSION Act of 2018. This act cleared the clutter and red tape to take care of one of America's greatest assets: veterans of the military who sacrificed so much to secure the country. The MISSION Act created the Veterans Community Care Program which allows veterans to choose to receive care at non-VA facilities when a VA facility is not available to them. This saves vets from long drives, having to wait too long for care, and when it is not in their best medical interest to receive care at a VA hospital. Veterans also have access to urgent care away from VA centers for the first time in history. This act puts veterans front and center in giving them the freedom for faster and better healthcare. Since signed into law, the MISSION Act has benefitted over 2.4 million veterans.[2]

One of Donald Trump's biggest campaign promises was to secure the borders of the United States and fix the immigration policies long plaguing the country. Once in office, President Trump wasted no time fulfilling his promise. Over 400 miles of high tech walls were built in the areas where the border was least secure. Trump sent nearly 5,000 troops to the border, working in conjunction with state and local governments, causing illegal crossings to plummet to historic lows. Where the walls were put up, crossings were down over 87 percent.[3] President Trump also vigorously worked to end catch and release; safely return asylum seekers to Mexico (fully enforcing the immigration laws of the United States, ending asylum fraud, and safeguarding migrant families); institute travel bans to keep out terrorists, jihadists, and violent extremists; and issue sanctions on countries refusing to take back their own nationals. Finally, there were issued regulations on combating "birth tourism."

Keeping America great means keeping America safe as well. Operation Legend was launched to tamp down violent crime in America's cities. Over 5,000 arrests were made. In 2019, violent crime dropped in this country for the third consecutive year, along with the murder rate decreasing by over 7 percent.[4] Knowing that neighborhoods are the solution to many problems, Project Safe Neighborhoods was revamped which brought together federal, state, local, and tribal law enforcement to fight violent crime. With police issues being front and center, President Trump signed an executive order to promote safe policing for communities to give local police departments incentive reforms. Donald Trump also created the first White House position focused solely on combating human trafficking.

With law enforcement comes justice, and Donald Trump then signed the bipartisan First Step Act into law, which was a landmark criminal justice bill designed to reduce repeat offending and help former inmates get back into society. The president promoted second chance hiring to get inmates back on their feet by providing them income in quality jobs along with a ready-to-work plan to connect employers with former inmates. On August 28, 2020, President Trump pardoned Anne Marie Johnson, a reformed inmate who is now a criminal justice reform advocate.

Sadly, one of the toughest tasks of being president is to represent the nation in times of national tragedy. Whether it be mass shootings, hurricanes, tornadoes, or wildfires, he is expected to be there for the American people. During President Trump's term in office, he responded to more of these than most. There were tragic mass shootings, hurricanes, tornadoes, and massive wildfires. As commander-in-chief, President Trump visited the victims as often as he could.

---

2   ("The True Legacy of Donald Trump" 2021)

3   (Trump Administration Accomplishments 2021)

4   (Trump Administration Accomplishments 2021)

On January 21, a new immigrant arrived on the shores of the United States—the novel coronavirus. On that day, a Washington state resident was the first in this country to be diagnosed with the coronavirus. The person in question had travelled home from Wuhan, China. The NIH, the CDC, and the Trump Administration carefully monitored the situation and prepared to take action. As the cases grew more numerous, primarily from people returning from Wuhan, China, action was taken. On January 29, the White House launched a Coronavirus Task Force concerned with keeping travelers from China outside the U.S. and getting citizens out of China. Two days later, President Trump declared a public health emergency. A mandatory fourteen-day quarantine was also imposed on U.S. citizens who had been in Hubei province in China. During this time, the White House began issuing travel warnings and travel bans. On Friday, March 13, 2019, President Trump signed the proclamation declaring a national emergency due to the coronavirus. In the State of the Union address, the president said he would "take all necessary steps to safeguard our citizens from the Virus." The task force and the president began working with industries to get personal protective gear distributed as quickly as possible, and contracted with Ford, General Motors, Phillips, and General Electric to produce ventilators, and other companies for N95 masks. The administration worked tirelessly to get what was needed, from beds and supplies to data management where it needed to be. Operation Warp Speed, the drive to speed the process for a vaccine, was enacted, utilizing all measures to produce a working vaccine. In all, there were thousands of things that needed to be done to safeguard the public during the crisis. Shortages of food, medical supplies, fuel, and everything needed to run the economy needed to be eliminated to keep the country running. Suddenly, the president was diagnosed with the virus, and was checked into Walter Reed Army Medical Center. President Trump continued to work while being treated, and returned to the White House as soon as possible.

Worldwide, President Trump worked tirelessly to restore America's leadership in the world and to balance the financial costs of leadership in NATO and other treaties. The administration secured $400 million in defense spending from NATO allies, and pushed for members who were not meeting their minimum obligations to step up. President Trump also received commitments from Japan and the Republic of Korea to assume more responsibility for their own defense. President Trump also pulled the nation from the disastrous Iran Nuclear Deal and enforced greater sanctions than ever on Iran. Always a history maker, President Trump was the first sitting president to meet with a leader of North Korea and to cross the demilitarized zone and enter North Korea.

President Trump brokered several historic peace accords and his administration performed the greatest diplomatic feat by a sitting president this century. The president fulfilled a campaign promise that other presidents promised but neglected to do. President Trump recognized Jerusalem as the capital of Israel and moved the American Embassy there. The president brokered historic normalization agreements between Israel and Sudan, the United Arab Emirates, and the Kingdom of Bahrain, for which he was nominated for the Nobel Peace Prize.

Due to Donald Trump's love for this country, he has inspired love and respect among his supporters, not seen in a leader since Ronald Reagan. President Trump has grown from a moneyed young man, real estate developer, hotelier, and reality TV star to fill the shoes of the penultimate accomplishment in this country: President of the United States. Since Donald Trump's term in office began, he donated his salary back to various departments of the federal government. Like every American president, the office takes its toll on the commander-in-chief. The daily stresses add weariness and fatigue like the tides wearing away the shoreline. Donald Trump did not need to be the president. He held no political office prior to being elected. Like the Roman Republicans of old the Founding Fathers sought to emulate, Mr. Trump stepped away from his holdings out of patriotism and love of his country to serve. To give back what was given to him. He endured the arrows and abuse many refused to. Let President Trump be an example for others citizen soldiers who step away to serve their country take the arrows and return to private life.

President Trump Hosts Turkey's President Erdogan at The White Hous

WASHINGTON, D.C. - MAY 16, 2017: U.S. President Donald Trump waits on the arrival of Turkish President Recep Tayyip Erdogan at the White House May 16, 2017 in Washington, D.C. (Photo by Win McNamee/Getty Images)

"If the freedom of speech is taken away then dumb and silent we may be led, like sheep to the slaughter."
George Washington

President Trump Addresses Conservative Political Action Conference

---

NATIONAL HARBOR, MD - MARCH 2, 2019 (AFP OUT): U.S. President Donald Trump hugs the U.S. flag during CPAC 2019 on March 2, 2019 in National Harbor, Maryland. (Photo by Tasos Katopodis/Getty Images)

President Trump Holds Campaign Rally in Fort Wayne, Indiana

FORT WAYNE, IN - NOVEMBER 5, 2018: U.S. President Donald Trump waves to the audience at a campaign rally for Republican Senate candidate Mike Braun at the County War Memorial Coliseum November 5, 2018 in Fort Wayne, Indiana.

(Photo by Aaron P. Bernstein/Getty Images)

Debates

*GOP Presidential Candidates Debate
in Milwaukee*

*Hillary Clinton and Donald Trump Face Off in First
Presidential Debate at Hofstra University*

MILWAUKEE, WI - NOVEMBER 10, 2015: Presidential candidate Donald Trump makes a face during the Fox Business and ***Wall Street Journal*** Presidential Debate at the Milwaukee Theatre November 10, 2015 in Milwaukee, Wisconsin.

(Photo by Scott Olson/Getty Images)

HEMPSTEAD, NY - SEPTEMBER 26, 2016: Republican presidential nominee Donald Trump gives an incredulous look listening to Hillary Clinton speak at the Presidential Debate at Hofstra University on September 26, 2016 in Hempstead, New York. (Photo by Win McNamee/Getty Images)

Inauguration

WASHINGTON, D.C. - JANUARY 20, 2017: President-elect Donald Trump and his wife Melania depart from services at St. John's Church during his inauguration in Washington, D.C., January 20, 2017.
(Photo by REUTERS/Joshua Roberts)

WASHINGTON, D.C.- JANUARY 20, 2017: U.S. President Donald Trump takes the oath of office with his wife Melania, and children Barron, Donald Jr., Eric, Ivanka and Tiffany at his side, during his inauguration at the U.S. Capitol in Washington, D.C., January 20, 2017.
(Photo by REUTERS/Kevin Lamarque)

WASHINGTON, D.C. - JANUARY 20, 2017: President-elect Donald Trump walks to take his seat for the inaugural swearing-in ceremony at the U.S. Capitol in Washington, D.C., Friday, January 20, 2017.
(Official White House Photo by Shealah Craighead)

President Donald Trump Attends Inauguration
Freedom Ball

WASHINGTON, D.C. - JANUARY 20, 2017:
President Donald Trump and First Lady Melania
Trump dance at the Freedom Inaugural Ball at the
Washington Convention Center on January 20, 2017
in Washington, D.C.
(Photo by Aaron P. Bernstein/Getty Images)

Make America Great Again

HAMPTON, VA - MARCH 2, 2017: President Donald Trump salutes sailors before boarding Marine One on the PCU Gerald R. Ford, Newport News, Virginia en route to Langley Air Force Base, Hampton, Virginia on Thursday, March 2, 2017.
(Official White House Photo by Shealah Craighead)

PRINCE GEORGE'S COUNTY, MD - MAY 19, 2017: President Donald Trump salutes as he and First Lady Melania Trump arrive aboard Marine One, Friday, May 19, 2017, to Joint Base Andrews, Maryland, for the start of their overseas visit to Saudi Arabia, Israel, Rome, Brussels, and Taormina, Italy. (Official White House Photo by Shealah Craighead)

"Unlike the socialists, we believe in the rule of the people, not the rule of the unelected bureaucrats that don't know what they are doing. We believe in the dignity of the individual, not the iron grip of the state. Our regulatory reforms are vital, not only to the success of our economy, but the strength of our democracy, and the survival of liberty itself."

Donald Trump

WASHINGTON, D.C. - FEBRUARY 2, 2017: President Donald Trump and Vice President Mike Pence admire several Harley-Davidson bikes on the South Lawn driveway of the White House in Washington, D.C. President Trump hosted a lunch for Harley-Davidson executives, as well as union representatives for machinist and steel workers, in the Roosevelt Room of the White House on Thursday, February 2, 2017. (Official White House Photo by Shealah Craighead)

WASHINGTON, D.C. - MARCH 23, 2017: President Donald Trump is eastbound and down as he welcomes truckers and CEOs to the White House on Thursday, March 23, 2017, to discuss healthcare. (Official White House Photo by Benjamin Applebaum)

YPSILANTI, MI - MARCH 15, 2017: President Donald Trump delivers remarks on job creation in the automobile and manufacturing industries on Wednesday, March 15, 2017, at the American Center for Mobility in Ypsilanti, Michigan. (Official White House Photo by Shealah Craighead)

Buy American – Hire American

WASHINGTON, D.C. - JUNE 1, 2017: U.S. President Donald Trump announces his decision for the United States to pull out of the Paris Climate Agreement and level the playing field in the Rose Garden at the White House on June 1, 2017 in Washington, D.C. Trump pledged on the campaign trail to withdraw from the accord.

(Photo by Chip Somodevilla/Getty Images)

CEDAR RAPIDS, IA - JUNE 21, 2017: President Donald J. Trump visits Kirkwood Community College to observe new technology in agriculture on June 21, 2017. (Official White House Photo by Joyce N. Boghosian)

WASHINGTON, D.C. - JUNE 29, 2017: President Donald J. Trump calls for a look into nuclear energy policy and to unleash energy exports at the Department of Energy on June 29, 2017. (Official White House Photo by Andrea Hanks)

COUNCIL BLUFFS, IA - JUNE 11, 2019: President Donald J. Trump, joined by Agriculture Secretary Sonny Perdue, shakes hands with Iowa Governor Kim Reynolds after signing an Executive Order making changes to the E15 ethanol rule, during his visit Tuesday, June 11, 2019, to Southwest Iowa Renewable Energy Ethanol Plant in Council Bluffs, Iowa. (Official White House Photo by Shealah Craighead)

WASHINGTON, D.C. - OCTOBER 17, 2018: President Donald J. Trump, joined by Vice President Mike Pence and members of his Cabinet, meet with workers on "Cutting the Red Tape and Unleashing Economic Freedom" on Wednesday, October 17, 2018, in the Oval Office of the White House. (Official White House Photo by Shealah Craighead)

MONACA, PA - AUGUST 13, 2019: President Donald J. Trump delivers remarks on America's Energy Dominance and Manufacturing Revival Tuesday, August 13, 2019, at the Shell Pennsylvania Petrochemicals Complex in Monaca, Pennsylvania. (Official White House Photo by Tia Dufour)

PITTSBURG, PA - OCTOBER 23, 2019: President Donald J. Trump welcomes Andrea Brownlee, owner of Brownlee Trucking, to the stage to deliver remarks at the 9th Annual Shale Insight Conference on Wednesday, October 23, 2019, at the David L. Lawrence Convention Center in Pittsburgh. (Official White House Photo by Tia Dufour)

PEOTSA, IA - JULY 26, 2018: U.S. President Donald Trump holds up "Make Our Farmers Great Again!" hats as he arrives

for a roundtable discussion on workforce development at Northeast Iowa Community College in Peosta, Iowa, July 26, 2018.

(Photo by SAUL LOEB / AFP) (Photo by SAUL LOEB/AFP via Getty Images)499

SPRINGFIELD, MO - AUGUST 30, 2017: President Donald J. Trump participates in a tax reform kickoff event at the Loren Cook Company on Wednesday, August 30, 2017, in Springfield, Missouri. (Official White House Photo by Joyce N. Boghosian)

MONACA, PA - AUGUST 13, 2019: President Donald J. Trump is shown the expansion construction underway as he tours the Shell Pennsylvania Petrochemicals Complex on Tuesday, August 13, 2019, in Monaca, Pennsylvania. (Official White House Photo by Tia Dufour)

MIDLAND, TX - JULY 29, 2020: President Donald J. Trump, joined by Secretary of Interior David Bernhardt (left), Secretary of Energy Dan Brouillette, Senator Ted Cruz, U.S. Rep. Mike Conaway, R-Texas, and U.S. Rep. Jodey Arrington, R-Texas, signs presidential permits on Wednesday, July 29, 2020, at the Double Eagle Oil Rig in Midland, Texas. (Official White House Photo by Shealah Craighead)

WASHINGTON, D.C. - DECEMBER 12, 2018: President Donald J. Trump displays his signature on Wednesday, December 12, 2018, after signing the Executive Order to establish the White House Opportunity and Revitalization Council in the Roosevelt Room of the White House. (Official White House Photo by Tia Dufour)

WASHINGTON, D.C. - JUNE 5, 2020: President Donald J. Trump delivers remarks on the U.S. Labor Department's positive job gains report during a press conference on Friday, June 5, 2020, in the Rose Garden of the White House. (Official White House Photo by Tia Dufour)

WASHINGTON, D.C. - JANUARY 29, 2020: President Donald J. Trump greets invited guests following the signing ceremony for the United States-Mexico-Canada Trade Agreement on Wednesday, January 29, 2020, in front of the South Portico of the White House. (Official White House Photo by Shealah Craighead)

WASHINGTON, D.C. – JANUARY 29, 2020: President Donald J. Trump, joined by Vice President Mike Pence and U.S. Trade Representative Robert Lighthizer, walk through the Rose Garden en route to the signing ceremony for the United States-Mexico-Canada Trade Agreement on Wednesday, January 29, 2020, in front of the South Portico of the White House. (Official White House Photo by Shealah Craighead)

BUENOS AIRES, ARGENTINA - NOVEMBER 30, 2018: President Donald J. Trump is joined by Mexican President Enrique Pena Nieto and Canadian Prime Minister Justin Trudeau at the USMCA signing ceremony on Friday, November 30, 2018, in Buenos Aires, Argentina. (Official White House Photo by Shealah Craighead)

WASHINGTON, D.C. - AUGUST 2, 2019: President Donald J. Trump listens as cattle industry representatives deliver remarks on Friday, August 2, 2019, in the Roosevelt Room of the White House, at the announcement of an agreement between the U.S. and the European Union to increase U.S. beef exports to European markets. (Official White House Photo by Joyce N. Boghosian)

WASHINGTON, D.C. - AUGUST 2, 2019: President Donald J. Trump joins European Union Ambassador Stavros Lambrinidis, U.S. Trade Representative Ambassador Robert Lighthizer, and Jani Raappana of Finland representing the EU Presidency on Friday, August 2, 2019, in the Roosevelt Room of the White House, as agreements are signed between the U.S. and the European Union to increase U.S. beef exports to European markets. (Official White House Photo by Joyce N. Boghosian)

BUENOS AIRES, ARGENTINA - NOVEMBER 30, 2018: President Donald J. Trump and President Mauricio Macri of the Argentine Republic appear on stage during the G20 welcoming ceremony in Buenos Aires, Argentina. (Official White House Photo by Shealah Craighead)

BUENOS AIRES, ARGENTINA - DECEMBER 1, 2018: President Donald J. Trump participates in a bilateral meeting with German Chancellor Angela Merkel at the G20 Summit Saturday, December 1, 2018, in Buenos Aires, Argentina. (Official White House Photo by Shealah Craighead)

BUENOS AIRES, ARGENTINA - NOVEMBER 30, 2018: President Donald J. Trump participates in a trilateral meeting on Friday, November 30, 2018, with Japanese Prime Minister Shinzo Abe and India Prime Minister Narendra Modi at the G20 Summit in Buenos Aires, Argentina. (Official White House Photo by Shealah Craighead)

UENOS AIRES, ARGENTINA - NOVEMBER 30, 2018: President Donald J. Trump and First Lady Melania Trump are greeted by Argentine President Mauricio Macri and First Lady Juliana Awada upon their arrival Friday evening, November 30, 2018, at the Teatro Colon in Buenos Aires, Argentina. (Official White House Photo by Andrea Hanks)

BUENOS AIRES, ARGENTINA - NOVEMBER 30, 2018: President Donald J. Trump and First Lady Melania Trump, joined by fellow G20 leaders, spouses, and guests attend the cultural program at the Opera House Friday evening, November 30, 2018, at the Teatro Colon in Buenos Aires, Argentina. (Official White House Photo by Andrea Hanks)

BUENOS AIRES, ARGENTINA - NOVEMBER 30, 2018: President Donald J. Trump and First Lady Melania Trump join fellow G20 leaders, spouses, and guests Friday evening, November 30, 2018, at the Teatro Colon in Buenos Aires, Argentina. (Official White House Photo by Andrea Hanks)

CHAROLETTE, NC - SEPTEMBER 24, 2020: President Donald J. Trump, joined on stage by medical professionals and invited guests, signs an Executive Order protecting insurance for people with pre-existing medical conditions on Thursday, September 24, 2020, at the Duke Energy Hangar in Charlotte, North Carolina. (Official White House Photo by Shealah Craighead)

WASHINGTON, D.C. - OCTOBER 12, 2017: President Donald J. Trump signs the Executive Order to Promote Healthcare Choice and Competition on October 12, 2017. (Official White House Photo by Andrea Hanks)

WASHINGTON, D.C. - JUNE 24, 2020: President Donald J. Trump, joined by First Lady Melania Trump, displays his signature after signing an executive order on strengthening the child welfare system for America's children Wednesday, June 24, 2020, in the Oval Office of the White House. (Official White House Photo by Shealah Craighead)

WASHINGTON, D.C. - APRIL 29, 2019: President Donald J. Trump welcomes the 2019 National Teacher of the Year Award winners to the Oval Office Monday, April 29, 2019, at the White House. (Official White House Photo by Joyce N. Boghosian)

WASHINGTON, D.C. - DECEMBER 9, 2019: President Donald J. Trump, joined by Vice President Mike Pence, addresses his remarks at a roundtable on empowering families with education choice on Monday, December 9, 2019, in the Cabinet Room of the White House. (Official White House Photo by Tia Dufour)

ORLANDO, FL - MARCH 3, 2017: President Donald Trump and U.S. Secretary of Education Betsy DeVos participate in a tour of Saint Andrew's Catholic School on Friday, March 3, 2017, in Orlando, Florida. (Official White House Photo by Shealah Craighead)

PRINCE GEORGE'S COUNTY, MD - AUGUST 21, 2019: President Donald J. Trump boards Air Force One at Joint Base Andrews, Maryland. Wednesday, August 21, 2019, en route to Louisville International Airport in Louisville, Kentucky. (Official White House Photo by Shealah Craighead)

WASHINGTON, D.C. – FEBRUARY 5, 2019: U.S. President Donald Trump gestures before he delivers a State of the Union address to a joint session of Congress at the U.S. Capitol in Washington, D.C. on Tuesday, February 5, 2019. (Photo by Doug Mills/Pool via Bloomberg)

WASHINGTON, D.C. - FEBRUARY 28, 2017 (AFP OUT): U.S. Vice President Mike Pence (left) and Speaker of the House Paul Ryan (right) applaud as U.S. President Donald J. Trump (center) arrives to deliver his first address to a joint session of the U.S. Congress on February 28, 2017 in the House chamber of the U.S. Capitol in Washington, D.C. (Photo by Jim Lo Scalzo - Pool/Getty Images)

WASHINGTON, D.C. - FEBRUARY 4, 2020: President Donald J. Trump arrives in the House chamber and is greeted by members of Congress prior to delivering his State of the Union address on Tuesday, February 4, 2020 at the U.S. Capitol in Washington, D.C. (Official White House Photo by Andrea Hanks)

WASHINGTON, D.C. - JUNE 21, 2019: President Donald J. Trump, joined by First Lady Melania Trump, Vice President Mike Pence, and Second Lady Karen Pence, delivers remarks during the Congressional Picnic on Friday, June 21, 2019, on the Blue Room Balcony of the White House. (Official White House Photo by Andrea Hanks)

WASHINGTON, D.C. - JANUARY 2, 2019: President Donald J. Trump, joined by Vice President Mike Pence, Secretary of Homeland Security Kristjen Nielsen, Congressman Kevin McCarthy, and Congressman Steve Scalise, addresses his remarks from the Rose Garden of the White House following his meeting with Congressional leadership in the Situation Room Wednesday, January 2, 2019. (Official White House Photo by Tia Dufour)

PHILIDELPHIA, PA - JANUARY 26, 2017: President Donald Trump talks on the phone aboard Air Force One during a flight to Philadelphia, Pennsylvania, to address a joint gathering of House and Senate Republicans on Thursday, January 26, 2017. This was the President's first trip aboard Air Force One. (Official White House Photo by Shealah Craighead)

WASHINGTON, D.C. - JUNE 21, 2019: President Donald J. Trump, joined by First Lady Melania Trump, Vice President Mike Pence, and Second Lady Karen Pence, June 21, 2019, on the Blue Room Balcony of the White House. (Official White House Photo by Andrea Hanks)

VATICAN CITY - MAY 24, 2017: President Donald Trump and First Lady Melania Trump tour the Sistine Chapel following their meeting with His Holiness Pope Francis on Wednesday, May 24, 2017, in Vatican City.

(Official White House Photo by Andrea Hanks)

WASHINGTON, D.C. - APRIL 23, 2021: Members of the Supreme Court pose for a group photo at the Supreme Court in Washington, D.C. on April 23, 2021. Seated from left: Associate Justice Samuel Alito, Associate Justice Clarence Thomas, Chief Justice John Roberts, Associate Justice Stephen Breyer, and Associate Justice Sonia Sotomayor. Standing from left: Associate Justice Brett Kavanaugh, Associate Justice Elena Kagan, Associate Justice Neil Gorsuch, and Associate Justice Amy Coney Barrett. (Photo by Erin Schaff-Pool/Getty Images)

WASHINGTON, D.C. - JANUARY 31, 2017: President Donald Trump joins Judge Neil M. Gorsuch, Louise Gorsuch, and others in prayer in the Green Room of the White House in Washington, D.C., following the President's announcement of Judge Gorsuch as his nominee to the Supreme Court on Tuesday January 31, 2017. (Official White House Photo by Shealah Craighead)

WASHINGTON, D.C. - OCTOBER 8, 2018: President Donald J. Trump looks on as Anthony M. Kennedy—retired Associate Justice of the Supreme Court of the United States—swears in Judge Brett M. Kavanaugh to be the Supreme Court's 114th justice on Monday, October 8, 2018, in the East Room of the White House in Washington, D.C. Justice Kavanaugh is joined by his wife Ashley, holding the Bible, and their daughters Liza and Margaret. (Official White House Photo by Joyce N. Boghosian)

WASHINGTON, D.C. - SEPTEMBER 26, 2020: President Donald J. Trump and First Lady Melania Trump, joined by White House senior advisors, pose for a photo with Judge Amy Coney Barrett, the president's nominee for Associate Justice of the Supreme Court of the United States, her husband Jesse, and their children on Saturday, September 26, 2020, in the Oval Office of the White House. (Official White House Photo by Andrea Hanks)

PRINCE GEORGE'S COUNTY, MD - NOVEMBER 6, 2019: President Donald J. Trump disembarks Marine One at Joint Base Andrews, Maryland on Wednesday, November 6, 2019, and is escorted to Air Force One by U.S. Air Force Col. Rebecca J. Sonkiss. (Official White House Photo by Joyce N. Boghosian)

U.S. AIR FORCE ACADEMY, CO - MAY 30, 2019: President Donald Trump arrives at the Air Force Academy for the 2019 Graduation Ceremony. (U.S. Air Force photo/Joshua Armstrong)

U.S. AIR FORCE ACADEMY, CO - MAY 30, 2019: President Donald Trump congratulates a graduating cadet at the U.S. Air Force Academy Graduation Ceremony. (U.S. Air Force photo/Joshua Armstrong)

U.S. AIR FORCE ACADEMY, CO - MAY 30, 2019: President Trump congratulates Cadet 1st Class Trey Landon Arnold, the top graduating cadet, during the U.S. Air Force Academy Class of 2019 Graduation Ceremony at the Academy's Falcon Stadium in Colorado Springs, Colorado, May 30, 2019. Nine hundred and eighty-nine cadets crossed the stage to become the Air Force's newest second lieutenants. (U.S. Air Force photo/ Joshua Armstrong)

U.S. AIR FORCE ACADEMY, CO - MAY 30, 2019: USAF Graduation shot—hugs all around for an incredible achievement as the President congratulates other graduates.

U.S. AIR FORCE ACADEMY, CO - NOVEMBER 10, 2017: President Donald J. Trump departs China. Trump takes time out for a picture with the Marine Embassy guards on November 10, 2017. (Official White House Photo by Shealah Craighead)

ANCHORAGE, AK - JUNE 26, 2019: President Donald J. Trump poses for photos, shakes hands, and signs autographs with military personnel on Wednesday, June 26, 2019, during a refueling stop at Joint Base Elmendorf in Anchorage, Alaska. President Trump is traveling to attend the G20 Summit in Osaka, Japan. (Official White House Photo by Shealah Craighead)

WASHINGTON, D.C. - NOVEMBER 15, 2018: President Donald J. Trump and First Lady Melania Trump visit with Marines at the Marine Barracks Thursday, November 15, 2018, in Washington, D.C. (Official White House Photo by Andrea Hanks)

NEW LONDON, CT - MAY 17, 2017: U.S. President Donald Trump delivers the commencement address at the commence-ment ceremony at the U.S. Coast Guard Academy, May 17, 2017 in New London, Connecticut. This is President Trump's second commencement address since taking office and comes amid controversy after his firing of FBI Director James Comey.

(Photo by Drew Angerer/Getty Images)

WASHINGTON, D.C. - OCTOBER 26, 2019: President Donald J. Trump is joined by Vice President Mike Pence, National Security Advisor Robert O'Brien (left), Secretary of Defense Mark Esper, and Chairman of the Joint Chiefs of Staff U.S. Army General Mark A. Milley, (right) on Saturday, October 26, 2019, in the Situation Room of the White House monitoring developments as U.S. Special Operations forces close in on notorious ISIS leader Abu Bakr al-Baghdadi's compound in Syria with a mission to kill or capture the terrorist. (Official White House Photo by Shealah Craighead)

WASHINGTON, D.C. - NOVEMBER 25, 2019: President Donald J. Trump welcomes Conan, the military working dog, to the Oval Office Monday, November 25, 2019, at the White House. Conan participated in the military operation targeting ISIS leader Abu Bakr al-Baghdadi. (Official White House Photo by Shealah Ctraighead)

ARLINGTON, VA - SEPTEMBER 11, 2019: President Donald J. Trump and First Lady Melania Trump attend the September 11th Pentagon Observance Ceremony Wednesday, September 11, 2019, at the Pentagon in Arlington, Virginia. (Official White House Photo by Shealah Craighead)

Nasa and Space Force

ORLANDO, FL - MAY 27, 2020: President Donald J. Trump and First Lady Melania Trump disembark Air Force One at the NASA Shuttle Landing Facility on Wednesday, May 27, 2020, in Orlando, Florida.

(Official White House Photo by Andrea Hanks)

WASHINGTON, D.C. - OCTOBER 18, 2019: President Donald J. Trump, joined by Vice President Mike Pence, Presidential Advisor Ivanka Trump, and NASA Administrator Jim Bridenstine, talks via video teleconference with NASA astronauts Jessica Meir and Christina Koch during the first all-women's spacewalk Friday, October 18, 2019, from the Roosevelt Room of the White House. (Official White House Photo by Joyce N. Boghosian)

CAPE CANAVERAL, FL - MAY 27, 2020: President Donald J. Trump, First Lady Melania Trump, Vice President Mike Pence, and Second Lady Karen Pence pose for a photo with Lockheed Martin Vice President and Orion Project Manager Michael Hawes, Lockheed Martin CEO Marillyn Hewson, NASA Administrator Jim Bridenstine, and Kennedy Space Center Director Bob Cabana during a tour of the Orion capsules on Wednesday, May 27, 2020, at the Kennedy Space Center Operational Support Building in Cape Canaveral, Florida. (Official White House Photo by Andrea Hanks)

PRINCE GEORGE'S COUNTY, MD - DECEMBER 20, 2019: President Donald J. Trump greets Gen. Jay Raymond after being named the first Chief of Space Operations and first member of the United States Space Force on Friday, December 20, 2019, at Hangar 6 at Joint Base Andrews, Maryland. (Official White House Photo by Shealah Craighead)

WASHINGTON, D.C. - MAY 15, 2020: U.S. Space Force CSO Gen. Jay Raymond and U.S. Space Force Senior Enlisted Advisor CMSgt Roger Towberman present President Donald J. Trump with the U.S. Space Force Flag on Thursday, May 15, 2020, in the Oval Office of the White House. (Official White House Photo by Shealah Craighead)

PRINCE GEORGE'S COUNTY, MD - DECEMBER 20, 2019: President Donald J. Trump and First Lady Melania Trump depart Hangar 6 at Joint Base Andrews, Maryland on Friday, December 20, 2019, after signing S. 1790, The National Defense Authorization Act for Fiscal Year 2020. (Official White House Photo by Shealah Craighead)

PORTSMOUTH, ENGLAND - JUNE 5, 2019: Queen Elizabeth II and U.S. President Donald Trump attend the D-Day75 National Commemorative Event to mark the 75th Anniversary of the D-Day Landings at Southsea Common on June 5, 2019 in Portsmouth, England. (Photo by Karwai Tang/WireImage)

PARIS, FRANCE - NOVEMEBER 11, 2018: President Donald J. Trump and First Lady Melania Trump attend the Centennial of the 1918 Armistice Day ceremony on Sunday, November 11, 2018, at the Arc de Triomphe in Paris. (Official White House Photo by Shealah Craighead)

WASHINGTON, D.C. - JULY 25, 2017: President Donald J. Trump honors veteran Bob Bishop at the AMVETS Post 44 Salute to American Heroes on July 25, 2017. (Official White House Photo by Shealah Craighead)

SURESNES, FRANCE - NOVEMBER 11, 2018: President Donald J. Trump is at the American Commemoration Ceremony at Suresnes American Cemetery on Sunday, November 11, 2018. (Official White House Photo by Shealah Craighead)

*WASHINGTON, D.C. - MAY 13, 2019: President Donald J. Trump welcomes retired U.S. Marine Sgt. John Peck back to the Oval Office of the White House Monday, May 13, 2019, where Peck presented President Trump with a copy of his newly released book, **Rebuilding Sergeant Peck**. Peck—who lost his arms and legs following an IED explosion in Afghanistan in 2010—first met President Trump at the Walter Reed Military Medical Center in 2017. (Official White House Photo by Tia Dufour)*

WASHINGTON, D.C. - NOVEMBER 25, 2019: President Donald J. Trump displays his signature after signing S.153, The Supporting Veterans in STEM Careers Act, in the Oval Office of the White House. (Official White House Photo by Tia Dufour)

WASHINGTON, D.C. - JULY 27, 2020: President Donald J. Trump and Veterans Affairs Secretary Robert Wilkie pose with Second Lady Karen Pence and U.S. Marine Terry Sharpe on Monday, July 27, 2020, outside the South Portico entrance of the White House. Mr. Sharpe walked from North Carolina to Washington D.C. to raise awareness of veteran suicides. (Official White House Photo by Delano Scott)

WASHINGTON, D.C. - MARCH 21, 2020: President Donald J. Trump signs S. 3503, "A bill to authorize the Secretary of Veterans Affairs to treat certain programs of education converted to distance learning by reason of emergencies and health-related situations in the same manner as programs of education pursued at educational institutions, and for other purposes," on Saturday, March 21, 2020, in the Oval Office of the White House. (Official White House Photo by Tia Dufour)

Border Security and Law Enforcement

BETHPAGE, NY - MAY 21, 2018: U.S. President Donald Trump speaks alongside Evelyn Rodriguez (left), whose daughter was killed by MS-13 gang members, during a roundtable discussion on immigration at Morrelly Homeland Security Center in Bethpage, New York on May 23, 2018. (Photo by SAUL LOEB/AFP via Getty Images)

WASHINGTON, D.C. - JANUARY 25, 2017: President Donald Trump displays a signed Executive Order at the Department of Homeland Security in Washington, D.C., Wednesday, January 25, 2017. President Trump signed two Executive Orders to aid in border security and immigration enforcement improvements, and to enhance public safety in the interior of the United States. (Official White House Photo by Shealah Craighead)

SAN DIEGO, CA - SEPTEMBER 18, 2019: President Donald J. Trump signs a section of border fencing during his visit to the border area of Otay Mesa on Wednesday, September 18, 2019—a neighborhood along the Mexican border in San Diego, California. (Official White House Photo by Shealah Craighead)

MCALLEN, TX - JANUARY 10, 2019: President Donald J. Trump poses for a photo with U.S. Customs and Border Protection officers, legislators, and Department of Homeland Security Secretary Kirstjen Nielsen at an overlook along the Rio Grande following a briefing on Immigration and Border Security on Thursday, January 10, 2019, near the U.S. Border Patrol McAllen Station in McAllen, Texas. (Official White House Photo by Shealah Craighead)

MCALLEN, TX - JANUARY 10, 2019: President Donald J. Trump poses for a photo with U.S. Customs and Border Protection officers, legislators, and Department of Homeland Security Secretary Kirstjen Nielsen at an overlook along the Rio Grande following a briefing on Immigration and Border Security on Thursday, January 10, 2019, near the U.S. Border Patrol McAllen Station in McAllen, Texas. (Official White House Photo by Shealah Craighead)

YUMA, AZ - JUNE 23, 2020: President Donald J. Trump walks along the completed 200th mile of new border wall on Tuesday, June 23, 2020, along the U.S.-Mexico border near Yuma, Arizona. (Official White House Photo by Shealah Craighead)

WASHINGTON, D.C. - NOVEMBER 9, 2018: President Donald J. Trump signs an Immigration Proclamation declaring that migrants seeking asylum along the southern border must present themselves lawfully at a port of entry on Friday, November 9, 2018, in the Diplomatic Reception Room of the White House. (Official White House Photo by Joyce N. Boghosian)

SAN DIEGO, CA - SEPTEMBER 18, 2019: President Donald J. Trump visits the border area of Otay Mesa on Wednesday, September 18, 2019—a neighborhood along the Mexican border in San Diego, California. (Official White House Photo by Shealah Craighead)

MCALLEN, TX - JANUARY 10, 2019: President Donald J. Trump speaks with U.S. Customs and Border Protection officers coming in for their shift change, after President Trump attended a Roundtable on Immigration and Border Security Thursday, January 10, 2019, at the U.S. Border Patrol McAllen Station in McAllen, Texas. (Official White House Photo by Shealah Craighead)

WASHINGTON, D.C. - JULY 1, 2019: President Donald J. Trump, joined by Vice President Mike Pence and Health and Human Services Secretary Alex Azar, signs H.R. 3401, the Emergency Supplemental Appropriations for Humanitarian Assistance and Security at the Southern Border Act of 2019 on Monday, July 1, 2019, in the Oval Office of the White House. (Official White House Photo Joyce N. Boghosian)

ALAMO, TX - JANUARY 12, 2021: President Donald J. Trump delivers remarks at the 450th mile of the new border wall on Tuesday, January 12, 2021, near the Texas-Mexico border. (Official White House Photo by Shealah Craighead)

WASHINGTON, D.C. - JANUARY 31, 2020: President Donald J. Trump signs an Executive Order for Combating Human Trafficking and Online Child Exploitation in the United States, at the White House Summit on Human Trafficking in honor of the 20th Anniversary of the Trafficking Victims Protection Act of 2000 on Friday, January 31, 2020, in the East Room of the White House. (Official White House Photo by Tia Dufour)

KENOSHA, WI - SEPTEMBER 1, 2020: President Donald J. Trump is joined by U.S. Attorney William Barr (left), Rep. Bryan Steil, R- Wis., Senator Ron Johnson. R-Wis., and law enforcement officials as he concludes his tour at the emergency operation center Tuesday, September 1, 2020, at Mary D. Bradford High School in Kenosha, Wisconsin. (Official White House Photo by Shealah Craighead)

WASHINGTON, D.C. - MAY 15, 2019: President Donald J. Trump attends the 38th annual National Peace Officers' Memorial Service Wednesday, May 15, 2019, at the U.S. Capitol in Washington, D.C. (Official White House Photo by Shealah Craighead)

WASHINGTON, D.C. - JUNE 8, 2020: President Donald J. Trump and Vice President Mike Pence listen as Pat Yoes—the National President of the Fraternal Order of Police—addresses his remarks at a roundtable with Law Enforcement members on Monday, June 8, 2020, in the State Dining Room of the White House. (Official White House Photo by D. Myles Cullen)

CHICAGO, IL - OCTOBER 28, 2019: President Donald J. Trump, joined by Attorney General William Barr, prepares to sign an executive order on the Commission on Law enforcement and the Administration of Justice on Monday, October 28, 2019, following his remarks during the International Association of Chiefs of Police Annual Conference and Exposition at the McCormick Place Convention Center Chicago in Chicago. (Official White House Photo: Shealah Craighead)

BILOXI, MS - NOVEMBER 26, 2018: President Donald J. Trump, joined by Vice President Mike Pence and U.S. Senator Cindy Hyde-Smith, R-Miss., participates in the First Step Roundtable with Mississippi Gov. Phil Bryan and law enforcement leaders Monday, November 26, 2018, at the Mississippi Coast Coliseum in Biloxi, Mississippi. (Official White House Photo by D. Myles)

WASHINGTON, DC - JUNE 5, 2020: U.S. President Donald Trump shushes journalists before signing the Paycheck Protection Program Flexibility Act in the Rose Garden at the White House June 5, 2020 in Washington, D.C. The U.S. Labor Department announced the unemployment rate fell to 13.3 percent in May, a surprising improvement in the nation's job market, as hiring rebounded faster than economists expected in the wake of the novel coronavirus pandemic.

(Photo by Chip Somodevilla/Getty Images)

WASHINGTON, D.C. - AUGUST 28, 2020: President Donald J. Trump, joined by Alice Marie Johnson, whose life sentence was commuted by President Trump in 2019, announces to reporters that he is granting a full pardon to Johnson on Friday, August 28, 2020, in the Oval Office at the White House. (Official White House Photo by Tia Dufour)

WASHINGTON, D.C. - FEBRUARY 21, 2019: President Donald J. Trump and First Lady Melania Trump look on as Catherine Toney delivers remarks at the African American History Month Reception on Thursday, February 21, 2019, in the East Room of the White House. Toney was one of the first women released under the First Step Act. (Official White House Photo by Andrea Hanks)

WASHINGTON, D.C. - APRIL 1, 2019: President Donald J. Trump welcomes former federal inmate and now Georgetown University Law Center faculty member Shon Hopwood on stage Monday, April 1, 2019, at the 2019 Prison Reform Summit and First Step Celebration in the East Room of the White House. (Official White House Photo by Joyce N. Boghosian)

WASHINGTON, D.C. - APRIL 1, 2019: President Donald J. Trump addresses his remarks on Monday, April 1, 2019, at the 2019 Prison Reform Summit and First Step Celebration in the East Room of the White House, urging employers to institute second chance hiring practices. (Official White House Photo by Joyce N. Boghosian)

WASHINGTON, D.C. - APRIL 1, 2019: President Donald J. Trump congratulates former inmates on stage who have benefited from the First Step legislation on Monday, April 1, 2019, at the 2019 Prison Reform Summit and First Step Celebration in the East Room of the White House. (Official White House Photo by Joyce N. Boghosian)

YUBA COUNTY, CA - NOVEMBER 17, 2018: President Donald J. Trump disembarks Air Force One at Beale Air Force Base, California, Saturday, November 17, 2018, to begin his visit to Paradise, California, which was devastated by wildfires.

(Official White House Photo by Shealah Craighead)

PITTSBURG, PA - OCTOBER 30, 2018: President Donald J. Trump and First Lady Melania Trump, joined by Jared Kushner and Ivanka Trump, walk to a memorial on Tuesday, October 30, 2018, at the Tree of Life Congregation Synagogue in Pittsburgh, to remember the victims of Saturday's mass shooting. (Official White House Photo by Shealah Craighead)

WASHINGTON, D.C. - SEPTEMBER 1, 2019: President Donald J. Trump, joined by White House Homeland Security Advisor Admiral Pete Brown, talks to members of the press about Hurricane Dorian and the mass shooting near Odessa, Texas, as he returns to the White House Sunday, September, 1, 2019, from Camp David near Thurmont, Maryland. President Trump will attend an update briefing Sunday on Hurricane Dorian at the Federal Emergency Management Agency (FEMA) headquarters in Washington, D.C. (Official White House Photo by Joyce N. Boghosian)

EL PASO, TX - AUGUST 7, 2019: President Donald J. Trump and First Lady Melania Trump express their condolences to the family of shooting victims Jordan and Andre Anchondo, as she and President Trump met the Anchondo's two-month-old son who survived on Wednesday, August 7, 2019, at the University Medical Center of El Paso in El Paso, Texas. Jordan and Andre Anchondo were among the twenty-two people killed in a mass shooting Saturday at a Walmart in El Paso. (Official White House Photo by Andrea Hanks)

WASHINGTON, D.C. - NOVEMBER 14, 2018: President Donald J. Trump speaks on the phone in the Oval Office on Wednesday, November 14, 2018, with Federal Emergency Management Agency Administrator Brock Long to receive the latest update on the devastating wildfires in California. (Official White House Photo by Joyce N. Boghosian)

PARADISE, CA - NOVEMBER 17, 2018: President Donald J. Trump, is joined by California Governor Jerry Brown, Governor-elect Gavin Newsom, FEMA Administrator Brock Long, and Paradise, California Mayor Jody Jones, as he survey's the fire damage to the Skyway Villa Mobile Home and RV Park Saturday, November 17, 2018, in Paradise, California, which was devastated by the camp fire. (Official White House Photo by Shealah Craighead)

MACON, GA - OCTOBER 15, 2018: President Donald J. Trump and First Lady Melania Trump meet with local farmers to discuss the impact Hurricane Michael has had on their crops Monday, October 15, 2018, at Charlie Stewart's Farm in Macon, Georgia. (Official White House Photo by Andrea Hanks)

MACON, GA - OCTOBER 15, 2018: President Donald J. Trump and First Lady Melania Trump meet with local farmers to discuss the impact Hurricane Michael has had on their crops Monday, October 15, 2018, at Charlie Stewart's Farm in Macon, Georgia. (Official White House Photo by Andrea Hanks)

OPELIKA, AL - MARCH 8, 2019: President Donald J. Trump meets with residents affected by a tornado that touched down on Sunday in Opelika, Alabama Friday, March 8, 2019, at the disaster relief center at the Providence Baptist Church Annex Building in Opelika, Alabama. (Official White House Photo by Shealah Craighead)

ORANGE, TX - AUGUST 29, 2020: President Donald J. Trump participates in an emergency operations center briefing at the Orange County Convention and Expo Center in Orange, Texas, Saturday, August 29, 2020, as part of President Trump's visit to areas impacted by Hurricane Laura. (Official White House Photo by Shealah Craighead)

WASHINGTON, D.C. - SEPTEMBER 1, 2019: President Donald J. Trump, joined by Acting Secretary of the Department of Homeland Security Kevin McAleenan and Acting FEMA Administrator Pete Gaynor, attends a briefing on Sunday, September 1, 2019, on the current directional forecast of Hurricane Dorian at the Federal Emergency Management Agency (FEMA) headquarters in Washington, D.C. (Official White House Photo by Shealah Craighead)

BETHESDA, MD - OCTOBER 1, 2020: President Donald J. Trump works in the Presidential Suite at Walter Reed National Military Medical Center in Bethesda, Maryland on Saturday, October 3, 2020, after testing positive for COVID-19 on Thursday, October 1, 2020. (Official White House Photo by Joyce N. Boghosian)

WASHINGTON, D.C. - MARCH 6, 2020: President Donald J. Trump, joined by Secretary of Health and Human Services Alex Azar, signs the congressional funding bill for coronavirus response on Friday, March 6, 2020, in the Diplomatic Reception Room of the White House. (Official White House Photo by Tia Dufour)

WASHINGTON, D.C. - APRIL 16, 2020: President Donald J. Trump presents American Trucking Associations truck driver Stephen Richardson with a commemorative key on the South Lawn of the White House on Thursday, April 16, 2020, during an event recognizing the front line efforts of truck drivers during the COVID-19 crisis. (Official White House Photo by Joyce N. Boghosian)

WASHINGTON, D.C. - APRIL 3, 2020: President Donald J. Trump participates in a roundtable meeting with energy sector executives in the Cabinet Room of the White House on Friday, April 3, 2020, to discuss declining oil prices in the time of the global coronavirus pandemic and the dispute between Russia and Saudi Arabia to reduce output. (Official White House Photo by Shealah Craighead)

WASHINGTON, D.C. - MARCH 26, 2020: President Donald J. Trump and Vice President Mike Pence are joined by Senate Majority Leader Mitch McConnell; House Minority Leader Rep. Kevin McCarthy; Secretary of the Treasury Steven Mnuchin; Secretary of Agriculture Sonny Perdue; Secretary of Labor Eugene Scalia; Secretary of Transportation Elaine Chao; USTR Ambassador Robert Lighthizer; Rep. Kevin Brady, R-Texas; Rep. Greg Walden, R-Ore.; Rep. Steve Chabot, R-Ohio; Assistant to the President and NEC Director Larry Kudlow; White House Director of Legislative Affairs Eric Ueland; White House Coronavirus Task Force Coordinator Ambassador Deborah Birx, and Task Force member Dr. Anthony Fauci, prior to President Trump signing the $2.2 trillion assistance package to help American workers, small businesses, and industries crippled by the economic disruption caused by the coronavirus (COVID-19) outbreak. (Official White House Photo by Shealah Craighead)

WASHINGTON, D.C. - DECEMBER 8, 2020: President Donald J. Trump, joined by Vice President Mike Pence and senior White House staff, displays his signature after signing an Executive Order ensuring that the American people have priority access to COVID-19 vaccines developed in the U.S. or procured by the U.S. Government, at the Operation Warp Speed Vaccine Summit on Tuesday, December 8, 2020, in the South Court Auditorium at the Eisenhower Executive Office Building at the White House. (Official White House Photo by Shealah Craighead)

WASHINGTON, D.C. - APRIL 14, 2020: President Donald J. Trump meets with health executives in the Cabinet Room of the White House on Tuesday, April 14, 2020, to discuss the dynamic ventilator reserve. (Official White House Photo by Shealah Craighead)

BETHESDA, MD - OCTOBER 4, 2020: President Donald J. Trump greets supporters during a drive by outside of Walter Reed National Military Medical Center on Sunday, October 4, 2020, in Bethesda, Maryland. (Official White House Photo by Tia Dufour)

WASHINGTON, D.C. - MARCH 13, 2020: President Donald J. Trump signs the proclamation declaring a national emergency concerning the novel coronavirus disease (COVID-19) outbreak on Friday, March 13, 2020, in the Oval Office of the White House. (Official White House Photo by Shealah Craighead)

WASHINGTON, D.C. - JULY 5, 2017: President Donald Trump speaks to the media before departing from the South Lawn with First Lady Melania Trump at The White House on July 5, 2017, in Washington, D.C. President Trump will travel to Warsaw, Poland and Hamburg, Germany. (Photo by Zach Gibson/Getty Images)

BRUSSELS, BELGIUM - MAY 24, 2017: President Donald Trump and First Lady Melania Trump are welcomed by Belgium Prime Minister Charles Michel, and his wife, Amélie Derbaudrenghien, on their arrival to Brussels International Airport in Brussels, Belgium. (Official White House Photo by Shealah Craighead)

PARIS, FRANCE - JULY 13, 2017: President Donald J. Trump and President Emmanuel Macron on July 13, 2017. (Official White House Photo by Shealah Craighead)

WARSAW, POLAND - JULY 6, 2017: President Donald J. Trump and President Andrzej Duda on July 6, 2017. (Official White House Photo by Shealah Craighead)

RIYADH, SAUDI ARABIA - MAY 21, 2017: President Donald Trump and King Salman bin Abdulaziz Al Saud of Saudi Arabia attend the meeting of the Leaders of the Cooperation Council for the Arab States of the Gulf Countries on Sunday, May 21, 2017 at the King Abdulaziz Conference Center in Riyadh, Saudi Arabia. (Official White House Photo by Shealah Craighead)

RIYADH, SAUDI ARABIA - MAY 21, 2017: President Donald Trump greets the President of Egypt, Abdel Fattah Al Sisi, prior to their bilateral meeting on Sunday, May 21, 2017 at the Ritz-Carlton Hotel in Riyadh, Saudi Arabia. (Official White House Photo by Shealah Craighead)

AHMEDABAD, INDIA - FEBRUARY 24, 2020: President Donald J. Trump addresses his remarks at the Namaste Trump Rally on Monday, February 24, 2020, at the Motera Stadium in Ahmedabad, India. (Official White House Photo by Shealah Craighead)

SEOUL, SOUTH KOREA - JUNE 30, 2019: President Donald J. Trump and Republic of South Korea President Moon Jae-in attend their first bilateral meeting at Blue House on Sunday, June 30, 2019 in Seoul. (Official White House Photo by Shealah Craighead)

WASHINGTON, D.C. - JANUARY 15, 2020: President Donald J. Trump participates in a signing ceremony of an agreement between the United States and China with Chinese Vice Premier Liu He on Wednesday, January 15, 2020, in the East Room of the White House. Vice President Mike Pence attends. (Official White House Photo by D. Myles Cullen)

WASHINGTON, D.C. - JUNE 20, 2019: President Donald J. Trump bids farewell as Canadian Prime Minister Justin Trudeau's vehicle leaves Thursday, June 20, 2019, from the West Wing Lobby entrance of the White House. (Official White House Photo by Shealah Craighead)

WATFORD, ENGLAND - DECEMBER 4, 2019: President Donald J. Trump participates in an official welcome ceremony on Wednesday, December 4, 2019, with the Secretary General of the North Atlantic Treaty Organization (NATO) Jens Stoltenberg and the British Prime Minister Boris Johnson at the 70th anniversary of NATO in Watford, Hertfordshire outside London. (Official White House Photo by Shealah Craighead)

WASHINGTON, D.C. - SEPTEMBER 20, 2019: Australian Prime Minister Scott Morrison addresses his remarks at the official State Visit welcome ceremony Friday, September 20, 2019, on the South Lawn of the White House. (Official White House Photo by Shealah Craighead)

PANMUNJOM, SOUTH KOREA - JUNE 30, 2019 (SOUTH KOREA OUT): A handout photo provided by Dong-A Ilbo of North Korean leader Kim Jong Un and U.S. President Donald Trump inside the demilitarized zone (DMZ) separating South and North Korea on June 30, 2019 in Panmunjom, South Korea. U.S. President Donald Trump made history on this occasion by being the only sitting U.S. President to step foot inside North Korea.

(Handout photo by Dong-A Ilbo via Getty Images/Getty Images)

LONDON, ENGLAND - DECEMBER 3, 2019: President Donald J. Trump is joined by U.S. Ambassador to Great Britain Woody Johnson, U.S. Ambassador to NATO Kay Bailey Hutchison, and senior White House staff at their breakfast with NATO Secretary General Jens Stoltenberg Tuesday, December 3, 2019, at Winfield House in London. (Official White House Photo by Shealah Craighead)

LONDON, ENGLAND - DECEMBER 3, 2019: President Donald J. Trump and First Lady Melania Trump pose for a photo in front of No. 10 Downing Street in London on Tuesday, December 3, 2019, prior to attending a reception in honor of the 70th anniversary of NATO. (Official White House Photo by Andrea Hanks)

WASHIGNTON, D.C. - FEBRAURY 7, 2019: President Donald J. Trump, joined by Advisor to the President Ivanka Trump, members of his Cabinet, and guests, addresses his remarks at the signing of National Security Presidential Memorandum to launch the "Women's Global Development and Prosperity Initiative" on Thursday, February 7, 2019, in the Oval Office of the White House. (Official White House Photo by Joyce N. Boghosian)

JERUSALEM, ISRAEL - MAY 22, 2017: President Donald Trump places a prayer in between the stone blocks of the Western Wall in Jerusalem on Monday, May 22, 2017. (Official White House Photo by Dan Hansen)

WASHINGTON, D.C. - SEPTEMBER 15, 2020: President Donald J. Trump participates in a working luncheon with the Minister of Foreign Affairs of Bahrain Dr. Abdullatif bin Rashid Al-Zayani, Israeli Prime Minister Benjamin Netanyahu, and the Minister of Foreign Affairs for the United Arab Emirates Abdullah bin Zayed Al Nahyan on Tuesday, September 15, 2020, in the State Dining Room of the White House. (Official White House Photo by Shealah Craighead)

WASHINGTON, D.C. - SEPTEMBER 15, 2020: President Donald J. Trump, Minister of Foreign Affairs of Bahrain Dr. Abdullatif bin Rashid Al-Zayani, Israeli Prime Minister Benjamin Netanyahu, and Minister of Foreign Affairs for the United Arab Emirates Abdullah bin Zayed Al Nahyan sign the Abraham Accords on Tuesday, September 15, 2020, on the South Lawn of the White House. (Official White House Photo by Joyce N. Boghosian)

WASHINGTON, D.C. - JANUARY 28, 2020: President Donald J. Trump delivers remarks with Israeli Prime Minister Benjamin Netanyahu on Tuesday, January 28, 2020, in the East Room of the White House to unveil details of the Trump Administration's Middle East Peace Plan. (Official White House Photo by Shealah Craighead)

ERUSALEM, ISRAEL - MAY 23, 2017: President Donald Trump delivers remarks on Tuesday, May 23, 2017 at the Israel Museum in Jerusalem. (Official White House Photo by Shealah Craighead)

WASHINGTON, D.C. - OCTOBER 23, 2020:
President Donald J. Trump participates in a phone call
with Sudanese Chairman of the Sovereignty Council
Abdel Fattah al-Burhan, Sudanese Prime Minister
Abdalla Hamdok, and Israeli Prime Minister Benjamin
Netanyahu, to discuss Sudan's historic progress towards
democracy with its recognition of Israel and opportuni-
ties to advance peace in the region Friday, October 23,
2020, in the Oval Office of the White House.
(Official White House Photo Tia Dufour)

NEW YORK CITY, NEW YORK - SEPTEMBER 24,
2019: President Donald J. Trump, joined by Secretary of
State Mike Pompeo (left), drops by a regional coordina-
tion meeting on the Middle East Strategic Alliance on
Tuesday, September 24, 2019 at the Lotte New York
Palace in New York City. (Official White House Photo
by Shealah Craighead)

KEYSTONE, SD - JULY 3, 2020: U.S. President Donald Trump arrives for the Independence Day events at Mount Rushmore
National Memorial in Keystone, South Dakota, July 3, 2020. (Photo by SAUL LOEB / AFP)
(Photo by SAUL LOEB/AFP via Getty Images)

WASHINGTON, D.C. - OCTOBER 28, 2018: President Donald J. Trump and First Lady Melania Trump hand out candy to children outside the South Portico entrance of the White House Sunday, October 28, 2018, at the 2018 White House Halloween event. (Official White House Photo by Andrea Hanks)

WASHINGTON, D.C. - NOVEMBER 20, 2018: President Donald J. Trump, joined by First Lady Melania Trump, pardons turkeys "Peas" and "Carrots" on Tuesday, November 20, 2018 during the traditional ceremony in the Rose Garden of the White House. (Official White House Photo by Amy Rossetti)

WASHINGTON, D.C. - NOVEMBER 19, 2018: President Donald J. Trump and First Lady Melania Trump receive the White House Christmas tree on Monday, November 19, 2018 at the North Portico of the White House. (Official White House Photo by Andrea Hanks)

WASHINGTON, D.C. - APRIL 22, 2019: President Donald J. Trump and First Lady Melania Trump stand on the South Portico balcony of the White House as they welcome guests Monday, April 22, 2019, to the 141st White House Easter Egg Roll. (Official White House Photo by Shealah Craighead)

WASHINGTON, D.C. - FEBRUARY 27, 2020: U.S. President Donald Trump (center) stands in a prayer circle with African-American leaders in the Cabinet Room of the White House in Washington, D.C. on February 27, 2020. (Photo by Nicholas Kamm / AFP) (Photo by NICHOLAS KAMM/AFP via Getty Images)

WASHINGTON, D.C. - DECEMBER 3, 2018: President Donald J. Trump, joined by First Lady Melania Trump, salutes at the casket of former President George H. W. Bush, as the First Couple pay their respects Monday, December 3, 2018, at the U.S. Capitol in Washington, D.C. (Official White House Photo by Shealah Craiughead)

WASHINGTON, D.C. - SEPTEMBER 24, 2020: President Donald J. Trump and First Lady Melania Trump pay their respects to Associate Justice Ruth Bader Ginsburg on Thursday, September 24, 2020, as she lies in repose at the U.S. Supreme Court in Washington, D.C. Justice Ginsburg passed away on Friday, September 18, 2020. (Official White House Photo by Andrea Hanks)

WASHINGTON, D.C. - NOVEMBER 16, 2018: President Donald J. Trump presents the Medal of Freedom to Maureen Scalia who accepted the medal posthumously on behalf of her husband Justice Antonin Scalia on Friday, November 16, 2018, in the East Room of the White House. (Official White House Photo by Joyce N. Boghosian)

WASHINGTON, D.C. - NOVEMBER 16, 2018: President Donald J. Trump presents the Medal of Freedom Friday, November 16, 2018, in the East Room of the White House to Alan Page—Hall of Fame football player and jurist on the Minnesota Supreme Court. (Official White House Photo by Andrea Hanks)

WASHINGTON, D.C. - NOVEMBER 16, 2018: President Donald J. Trump presents the Medal of Freedom to Thomas Stevens who accepted the medal posthumously on behalf of his grandfather Babe Ruth on Friday, November 16, 2018, in the East Room of the White House. (Official White House Photo by Joyce N. Boghosian)

WASHINGTON, D.C. - SEPTEMBER 15, 2017: Eleven-year-old Frank "FX" Giaccio (left) gets a pat on the back from

U.S. President Donald Trump (center) while mowing the grass in the Rose Garden of the White House September 15, 2017

in Washington, D.C. Giaccio, from Falls Church, Virginia, who runs a business called FX Mowing, wrote a letter to Trump

expressing admiration for Trump's business background and offered to mow the White House grass.

(Photo by Win McNamee/Getty Images)

WASHINGTON, D.C. - JUNE 21, 2019: President Donald J. Trump, joined by First Lady Melania Trump, Vice President Mike Pence, and Second Lady Karen Pence, takes time for a photo June 21, 2019, on the Blue Room Balcony of the White House. (Official White House Photo by Andrea Hanks)

WASHINGTON, D.C. - OCTOBER 11, 2019: President Donald J. Trump poses for a photo with Little League Softball World Championship Team North Carolina's Rowan Little League Friday, October 11, 2019, in the Oval Office of the White House. (Official White House Photo by Shealah Craighead)

ELKRIDGE, MD - MAY 15, 2020: President Donald J. Trump poses with members of Girl Scout Troop 744 of Elkridge, Maryland, after presenting them with his certificate of recognition at the Presidential Recognition Ceremony: Hard Work, Heroism, and Hope on Friday, May 15, 2020, in the Rose Garden of the White House. (Official White House Photo by Andrea Hanks)

DAYTONA BEACH, FL - FEBRUARY 16, 2020: President Donald J. Trump, joined by First Lady Melania Trump, delivers remarks before the start of the NASCAR Daytona 500 auto race Sunday, February 16, 2020, at Daytona International Speedway in Daytona Beach, Florida. (Official White House Photo by Tia Dufour)

WASHINGTON, D.C. JANUARY 14, 2019: President Donald J. Trump welcomes members of the press to the State Dining Room Monday, January 14, 2019, where the 2018 NCAA Football National Champions, the Clemson Tigers, will be welcomed with food from Domino's, McDonald's, Wendy's, and Burger King. (Official White House Photo by Joyce N. Boghosian)

WEST PALM BEACH, FL - APRIL 19, 2019: President Donald J. Trump and radio commentator Rush Limbaugh pose for a photo Friday, April 19, 2019, during their round of golf at the Trump International Golf Club in West Palm Beach, Florida. (Official White House Photo by Joyce N. Boghosian)

WASHINGTON, D.C. - JULY 23, 2020: President Donald J. Trump attends the opening day of Little League with Mariano Rivera Thursday, July 23, 2020, on the South Lawn of the White House. (Official White House Photo by Shealah Craighead)

OLD FORGE, PA - AUGUST 20, 2020: President Donald J. Trump makes a stop at the Arcaro and Genell Takeaway Kitchen—a pizza shop in Old Forge, Pennsylvania—Thursday, August 20, 2020, during President Trump's visit to Pennsylvania. (Official White House Photo by Tia Dufour)

WASHINGTON, D.C. - DECEMBER 18, 2019: President Donald J. Trump talks to visitors and White House staff members on the South Lawn of the White House on Wednesday, December 18, 2019, prior to boarding Marine One to begin his trip to Michigan. (Official White House Photo by Joyce N. Boghosian)

WASHINGTON, D.C. - OCTOBER 22, 2020: President Donald J. Trump and First Lady Melania Trump greet White House staff members waving American flags as they depart the South Portico entrance of the White House on Thursday, October 22, 2020, before boarding Marine One on the South Lawn to begin their trip to Nashville, Tennessee. (Official White House Photo by Tia Dufour)

WASHINGTON, D.C. - JANUARY 24, 2020: President Donald J. Trump delivers remarks at the 47th Annual March for Life gathering Friday, January 24, 2020, at the National Mall in Washington, D.C. (Official White House Photo by Tia Dufour)

CHICAGO, IL - OCTOBER 28, 2019: President Donald J. Trump disembarks Air Force Two Monday, October 28, 2019, at O'Hare International Airport in Chicago and is met by supporters. (Official White House Photo by Shealah Craighead)

MANCHESTER, NH - FEBRUARY 10, 2020: Supporters cheer as U.S. President Donald Trump arrives for a "Keep America Great" rally at Southern New Hampshire University Arena on February 10, 2020 in Manchester, New Hampshire.

(Photo by Drew Angerer/Getty Images)

WASHINGTON, D.C. - JULY 4, 2020: President Donald J. Trump and First Lady Melania Trump watch fireworks from the Truman Balcony of the White House Saturday, July 4, 2020, during the Salute to America event on the South Lawn.

(Official White House Photo by Andrea Hanks)